AHHHHH

I'M SO BORED!

ACTIVITY BOOK FOR TEENS

CREEPED OUT EDITION

MADE BY TEENS

INSTRUCTIONS

MAKE A MESS OF THIS BOOK!

PLAY WITH YOUR FRIENDS OR ALONE TO PASS THE TIME.

EACH GAME HAS INDIVIDUAL INSTRUCTIONS.

SOLUTIONS TO PUZZLES IN THE BACK OF THE BOOK

MOST OF ALL HAVE SOME FUN!

HANGMAN

THE GAME IS TYPICALLY PLAYED BETWEEN TWO PEOPLE.

1. ONE PERSON, THE 'HOST' CHOOSES A WORD AND MARKS THE LENGTH OF THE WORD ON THE GRID.

2. THE OTHER PLAYER HAS TO GUESS THE LETTERS IN THIS WORD/PHRASE BEFORE ALL THE PARTS OF THE HANGMAN ARE DRAWN.

IF THE PLAYER GUESSES CORRECTLY THE LETTER IS MARKED IN THE CORRECT PLACE, IF THE PLAYER GUESSES INCORRECTLY THE HOST DRAWS ANOTHER PART OF THE HANGMAN.

THE GAME CONTINUES UNTIL THE WORD/PHRASE IS GUESSED (ALL LETTERS ARE REVEALED) IN THIS CASE THE SECOND PERSON HAS WON

OR

ALL THE PARTS OF THE HANGMAN ARE DISPLAYED IN WHICH CASE THE SECOND PERSON HAS LOST.

WOULD YOU RATHER

TAKE TURNS WITH ANOTHER PLAYER OR MANY PLAYERS IN ANSWERING THOUGHT-PROVOKING QUESTIONS. THE BEST MOST CREATIVE ANSWER WINS A POINT

EACH PAGE (HAVING FOUR QUESTIONS EACH) CAN BE PLAYED AS A ROUND OR THE WHOLE GAME DEPENDING ON HOW LONG YOU WOULD LIKE TO PLAY

THE PLAYER WITH THE MOST POINTS WINS!

CATEGORIES

IN THIS GAME YOU HAVE TO TRY TO FIND WORDS IN DIFFERENT CATEGORIES STARTING WITH THE SAME LETTER AND BEAT YOUR RIVALS.

USE DICE TO COUNT THROUGH THE ALPHABET FOR A LETTER OR PICK ONE AT RANDOM.

MYSTIC MASH

M.A.S.H. IS A FORTUNE TELLING GAME.

THE NAME COMES FROM THE WORDS: MANSION, APARTMENT, SHACK, HOUSE.

1. LIST FOUR OR FIVE OPTIONS FOR EACH CATEGORY WITH PICKING A TERRIBLE LAST OPTION FOR EACH. THIS IS A SPECIAL HOLIDAY VACATION EDITION SO THINK ABOUT WHAT YOUR HOLIDAY COULD BE LIKE GOOD OR BAD.

2. YOU CAN HAVE A FRIEND DRAW A SPIRAL IN THE DEDICATED CIRCLE OR IF YOU ARE ALONE, CLOSE YOUR EYES WHILE YOU DRAW YOUR SPIRAL. RANDOMLY STOP AND COUNT THE NUMBER OF SPIRAL LINES. THIS NUMBER WILL BE YOUR MAGIC NUMBER YOU CAN PUT IN THE HEART.

3. COUNT THROUGH EACH OF THE CATEGORIES UNTIL YOU REACH THE MAGIC NUMBER.

START FROM THE M AT THE TOP AND MOVING CLOCKWISE COUNTING EACH

OPTION UNTIL YOU REACH THE MAGIC NUMBER. CROSS OF THE OPTIONS YOU HAVE LANDED ON UNTIL YOU REACH ONE REMAINING OPTION. DO THIS FOR EACH CATEGORY LEAVING ONE FOR EACH.

4. READ EACH CATEGORY REVEALING YOUR FORTUNE!

WORD SEARCH

1. THERE ARE 15 WORDS TO FIND IN EACH SEARCH. THESE WORDS CAN BE HORIZONTAL, VERTICAL, DIAGONAL, AND BACKWARDS.

2. SOMETIMES THERE WILL BE 2 WORDS PUT TOGETHER; IN THIS CASE THE SPACE WAS DELETED IN THE SEARCH.

EXAMPLE: PEP RALLY IN THE SEARCH WILL BE PEPRALLY

SUDOKU

SUDOKU IS A SINGLE PLAYER LOGIC PUZZLE USING NUMBERS. YOU ARE GIVEN A 9X9 GRID WITH NUMBERS IN RANDOM PLACES BASED OFF OF DIFFICULTY LEVEL.

THE OBJECT IS TO PLACE THE NUMBERS 1 THROUGH 9 SO THAT

1. EACH ROW AND COLUMN HAVE NUMBERS 1 THROUGH 9.

2. EACH BOX: 3X3 SQUARE HAVE NUMBERS 1 THROUGH 9.

3. WITH NO REPEATS IN THE SAME ROW, COLUMN, OR BOX.

WICKED WORDPLAY

ONCE UPON A _____ NIGHT, A GROUP OF _____ FRIENDS DECIDED TO THROW THE MOST _____ HALLOWEEN
                    ADJECTIVE   NUMBER   ADJECTIVE

PARTY IN THE _____ THEY HAD EVER SEEN. THEY SPENT DAYS PLANNING THE _____ EVENT, FROM DECORATING
              NOUN   ADJECTIVE

THE _____ WITH _____ AND _____ TO CHOOSING THE MOST _____ COSTUMES.
     NOUN   NOUN   NOUN   ADJECTIVE

AS THE CLOCK STRUCK _____ ON HALLOWEEN NIGHT, THE PARTY WAS IN FULL SWING. THE _____ MUSIC PLAYED,
                     NUMBER   ADJECTIVE

AND THE _____ WERE FILLED WITH THE SOUND OF _____ AND _____ . THERE WAS EVEN A _____
         NOUN   NOUN   NOUN   ADJECTIVE

_____ IN THE CORNER, WHERE GUESTS COULD TAKE _____ IN A CAULDRON AND MAKE _____ -SHAPED
 NOUN   PLURAL NOUN   NOUN

_____ .
 NOUN

EVERYONE'S COSTUMES WERE _____ , FROM THE _____ DRESSED AS A _____ TO THE _____ WHO
                          ADJECTIVE   NOUN   NOUN   NOUN

LOOKED LIKE A _____ FROM ANOTHER _____ . THERE WAS EVEN A _____ WHO HAD TRANSFORMED INTO A
               NOUN   NOUN   NOUN

_____ WITH _____ AND _____ WINGS.
 NOUN   ADJECTIVE NOUN   NOUN

THE HIGHLIGHT OF THE EVENING WAS THE _____ _____ CONTEST. GUESTS TOOK TURNS TELLING _____
                                      ADJECTIVE NOUN   ADJECTIVE

_____ AND TRYING TO _____ EACH OTHER OUT WITH _____ TALES OF _____ AND _____
 NOUN   VERB   ADJECTIVE   NOUN   NOUN

_____ . THE WINNER RECEIVED A _____ _____ FILLED WITH _____ .
 VERB   ADJECTIVE NOUN   NOUN

AS THE NIGHT GREW LATER, THE _____ DECIDED TO _____ THROUGH THE _____ _____ OUTSIDE.
                             NOUN   VERB   ADJECTIVE NOUN

WITH FLASHLIGHTS IN HAND, THEY EXPLORED THE _____ _____ , SEARCHING FOR _____ AND _____
                                            ADJECTIVE NOUN   NOUN   NOUN

_____ . THERE WERE _____ _____ AND _____ HANGING FROM THE _____ , MAKING IT FEEL
 VERB   ADJECTIVE NOUN   NOUN   NOUN

LIKE A _____ FROM A _____ _____ .
        NOUN   ADJECTIVE NOUN

AFTER THEIR _____ ADVENTURE, THE FRIENDS RETURNED TO THE _____ FOR _____ AND
             ADJECTIVE   NOUN   ADJECTIVE NOUN

_____ _____ . THEY DANCED UNTIL THE _____ BEGAN TO _____ IN THE _____ , AND THE
 ADJECTIVE NOUN   NOUN   VERB   NOUN

_____ HALLOWEEN PARTY CAME TO A _____ .
 ADJECTIVE   VERB

IT WAS A NIGHT FULL OF _____ MEMORIES, AND THE FRIENDS KNEW THEY WOULD TREASURE THESE _____
                        ADJECTIVE   ADJECTIVE

MOMENTS FOR YEARS TO COME.

CATEGORIES GAME

LETTER	MONSTER	COSTUME	SCENERY	MOVIE	CANDY	SCORE

NUMBER OF ROUNDS

TOTAL SCORE

WOULD YOU RATHER...

SPEND HALLOWEEN NIGHT AT A HAUNTED HOUSE ATTRACTION WITH YOUR FRIENDS

OR

EXPLORE A REAL ABANDONED AND SPOOKY LOCATION WITH A SMALL GROUP

• •

DRESS UP AS A CLASSIC HORROR MOVIE MONSTER (E.G., VAMPIRE, WEREWOLF)

OR

CREATE A UNIQUE AND ELABORATE COSTUME THAT NO ONE ELSE WILL HAVE AT THE PARTY

• •

GO TRICK-OR-TREATING WITH A GROUP OF FRIENDS, COLLECTING AS MUCH CANDY AS POSSIBLE,

OR

HOST A HALLOWEEN-THEMED MOVIE NIGHT WITH SCARY MOVIES AND DELICIOUS TREATS

• •

HAVE A PUMPKIN FOR A HEAD

OR

BAT WINGS FOR ARMS DURING THE ENTIRE HALLOWEEN SEASON

PUMPKIN CARVING

CREATE YOUR OWN JACK-O'-LANTERN

BONE CHILLING MAZE
1

START

FINISH

HANGMAN

WORD: _____

| A B C D E F G H I J K L M N |
| O P Q R S T U V W X Y Z |

WORD: _____

| A B C D E F G H I J K L M N |
| O P Q R S T U V W X Y Z |

WORD: _____

| A B C D E F G H I J K L M N |
| O P Q R S T U V W X Y Z |

WORD: _____

| A B C D E F G H I J K L M N |
| O P Q R S T U V W X Y Z |

WORD: _____

| A B C D E F G H I J K L M N |
| O P Q R S T U V W X Y Z |

WORD: _____

| A B C D E F G H I J K L M N |
| O P Q R S T U V W X Y Z |

RIP

MYSTIC M.A.S.H.

MANSION-APARTMENT- SHACK-HOUSE

MONSTER SPOUSE

1. _____
2. _____
3. _____
4. _____
5. _____

HAUNTED HOUSE LOCATION

1. _____
2. _____
3. _____
4. _____
5. _____

SPOOKY TRANSPORTATION

1. _____
2. _____
3. _____
4. _____
5. _____

CREEPY CRAWLY PET

1. _____
2. _____
3. _____
4. _____
5. _____

NUMBER OF KIDS

1. _____
2. _____
3. _____
4. _____
5. _____

FUTURE MORBID JOB

1. _____
2. _____
3. _____
4. _____
5. _____

SPIRAL CIRCLE

YOUR MAGIC NUMBER

WOULD YOU RATHER...

EAT A HANDFUL OF CANDY CORN THAT TASTES LIKE REAL CORN

OR

A CHOCOLATE BAR THAT TASTES LIKE GARLIC

. . . .

HAVE TO BOB FOR APPLES IN A POOL FILLED WITH MASHED POTATOES

OR

WEAR A COSTUME THAT SQUEAKS LOUDLY WITH EVERY STEP YOU TAKE

. . . .

HAVE A TRICK-OR-TREAT BAG THAT NEVER GETS FULL NO MATTER HOW MUCH CANDY YOU COLLECT

OR

A COSTUME THAT MAKES YOU INVISIBLE WHEN YOU PUT IT ON

. . . .

HAVE TO EAT ALL YOUR HALLOWEEN CANDY IN ONE SITTING

OR

GIVE IT ALL AWAY TO TRICK-OR-TREATERS AND HAVE NONE FOR YOURSELF

WORD SEARCH 1
PG-13 HORROR

S	T	C	Z	E	G	D	U	R	G	E	H	T	E
U	T	U	W	Q	L	X	J	M	H	C	W	U	Q
H	E	G	O	E	M	Q	N	T	Z	A	U	O	N
M	Y	N	S	L	O	I	A	N	G	L	U	S	L
U	A	I	R	L	Q	E	M	A	H	P	J	T	N
Q	L	R	E	E	R	S	Y	N	T	T	V	H	H
R	P	U	H	B	E	N	D	G	V	E	F	G	F
L	E	J	T	A	T	E	N	I	R	I	I	I	N
B	M	N	O	N	A	S	A	L	G	U	W	L	Q
O	O	O	E	N	W	H	C	A	C	Q	V	Q	T
D	C	C	H	A	K	T	Y	M	O	M	Q	L	M
Z	L	V	T	U	R	X	T	H	E	R	I	N	G
P	A	Z	G	X	A	I	M	F	R	E	A	K	Y
X	W	R	L	U	D	S	U	P	M	A	R	K	I

ANNABELLE	DON'T BREATHE	QUIET PLACE
CANDYMAN	FREAKY	SIXTH SENSE
COME PLAY	KRAMPUS	THE GRUDGE
CONJURING	LIGHTS OUT	THE OTHERS
DARK WATER	MALIGNANT	THE RING

 # EASY

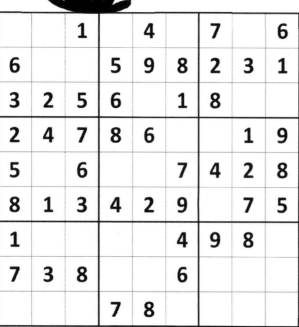

WOULD YOU RATHER....

TRICK-OR-TREAT DRESSED AS A GIANT RUBBER CHICKEN

OR

A DANCING TRAFFIC CONE

. . . .

HAVE TO SING "MONSTER MASH" EVERY TIME YOU MEET SOMEONE NEW ON HALLOWEEN

OR

DO THE THRILLER DANCE

. . . .

HAVE YOUR COSTUME ALWAYS BE ONE SIZE TOO SMALL

OR

ONE SIZE TOO BIG ON HALLOWEEN NIGHT

. . . .

BE CHASED BY A ZOMBIE HORDE

OR

CHASED BY A GANG OF FRIENDLY BUT OVERLY ENTHUSIASTIC TRICK-OR-TREATERS

CATEGORIES GAME

LETTER	MONSTER	COSTUME	SCENERY	MOVIE	CANDY	SCORE

NUMBER OF ROUNDS	TOTAL SCORE

HANGMAN

WORD: _____

ABCDEFGHIJKLMN
OPQRSTUVWXYZ

WORD: _____

ABCDEFGHIJKLMN
OPQRSTUVWXYZ

WORD: _____

ABCDEFGHIJKLMN
OPQRSTUVWXYZ

WORD: _____

ABCDEFGHIJKLMN
OPQRSTUVWXYZ

WORD: _____

ABCDEFGHIJKLMN
OPQRSTUVWXYZ

RIP

WORD: _____

ABCDEFGHIJKLMN
OPQRSTUVWXYZ

WICKED WORDPLAY

ON A _____ HALLOWEEN NIGHT, A GROUP OF _____ FRIENDS DRESSED AS _____ SET OUT FOR SOME EPIC TRICK-
ADJECTIVE · NUMBER · COSTUMES

OR-TREATING IN THEIR _____ NEIGHBORHOOD.
ADJECTIVE

THEIR FIRST STOP WAS A _____ HOUSE. THE DOOR CREAKED OPEN, REVEALING A _____ WITCH. SHE SAID,
SPOOKY · ADJECTIVE · ADJECTIVE

"SOLVE MY RIDDLE: WHAT DO GHOSTS USE TO _____ THEIR HAIR?"
VERB

THEY SHOUTED, "_____ SPRAY!" AND GOT A BAG OF _____ CANDY.
NOUN · ADJECTIVE

NEXT, THEY VISITED THE _____ GRAVEYARD, WHERE A _____ ZOMBIE YELLED, "TRICK OR _____!" THEY HANDED
ADJECTIVE · ADJECTIVE · VERB

OVER THEIR _____ AND RAN.
NOUN

AT A HAUNTED _____ A GHOST SAID, "_____ ME A _____, AND I'LL GIVE YOU A TREAT." THEY DREW A
NOUN · VERB · NOUN

_____ AND GOT _____.
NOUN · PLURAL NOUN

THEIR LAST STOP, A _____ MANSION, REVEALED A _____ VAMPIRE WHO LOVED _____. THEY EXCHANGED
ADJECTIVE · ADJECTIVE · NOUN

_____ FOR A _____ TREAT.
PLURAL NOUN · ADJECTIVE

WITH BAGS FULL OF _____, THEY HEADED HOME, SHARING _____ STORIES ABOUT THEIR HALLOWEEN ADVENTURE, A
PLURAL NOUN · ADJECTIVE

NIGHT THEY'D _____ FOR YEARS..
VERB

PUMPKIN CARVING

CREATE YOUR OWN JACK-O'-LANTERN

WORD SEARCH 2

HAUNTED HOUSE

```
S  U  N  T  W  J  M  W  X  Y  N  L  A  P
P  U  D  L  C  L  M  O  T  N  A  H  P  O
O  T  P  C  K  A  B  E  I  R  E  E  P  S
O  G  P  X  K  M  T  L  U  Y  Y  E  A  S
K  W  S  B  I  R  M  T  S  O  H  G  R  E
Y  O  T  G  D  O  A  A  A  A  I  O  I  S
G  O  I  D  E  N  O  D  N  A  B  A  T  S
U  N  R  B  R  A  H  Y  S  H  R  U  I  I
T  S  I  E  G  R  E  T  L  O  P  M  O  O
F  V  P  K  W  A  K  E  X  D  A  L  N  N
K  U  S  N  A  P  H  A  U  N  T  I  N  G
S  U  O  I  R  E  T  S  Y  M  R  B  W  E
I  P  F  Z  S  O  R  B  C  N  R  V  W  C
U  S  R  H  K  K  W  C  I  N  O  M  E  D
```

ABANDONED	GHOST	POLTERGEIST
APPARITION	HAUNTING	POSSESSION
CREAKING	MYSTERIOUS	SPIRITS
DEMONIC	PARANORMAL	SPOOKY
EERIE	PHANTOM	SUPERNATURAL

HANGMAN

WORD: _____

A B C D E F G H I J K L M N
O P Q R S T U V W X Y Z

WORD: _____

A B C D E F G H I J K L M N
O P Q R S T U V W X Y Z

WORD: _____

A B C D E F G H I J K L M N
O P Q R S T U V W X Y Z

WORD: _____

A B C D E F G H I J K L M N
O P Q R S T U V W X Y Z

WORD: _____

A B C D E F G H I J K L M N
O P Q R S T U V W X Y Z

WORD: _____

A B C D E F G H I J K L M N
O P Q R S T U V W X Y Z

RIP

MYSTIC M.A.S.H.

MANSION-APARTMENT- SHACK-HOUSE

MONSTER SPOUSE

1. _____
2. _____
3. _____
4. _____
5. _____

HAUNTED HOUSE LOCATION

1. _____
2. _____
3. _____
4. _____
5. _____

SPOOKY TRANSPORTATION

1. _____
2. _____
3. _____
4. _____
5. _____

CREEPY CRAWLY PET

1. _____
2. _____
3. _____
4. _____
5. _____

NUMBER OF KIDS

1. _____
2. _____
3. _____
4. _____
5. _____

FUTURE MORBID JOB

1. _____
2. _____
3. _____
4. _____
5. _____

SPIRAL CIRCLE

YOUR MAGIC NUMBER

CATEGORIES GAME

LETTER	MONSTER	COSTUME	SCENERY	MOVIE	CANDY	SCORE

NUMBER OF ROUNDS

TOTAL SCORE

WICKED WORDPLAY

IT WAS A DARK AND STORMY NIGHT, AND A GROUP OF_____ FRIENDS GATHERED IN A_____ IN THE MIDDLE OF
                                              ADJECTIVE   NOUN

NOWHERE. THE WIND HOWLED LIKE A_____ AS THEY TOLD_____ STORIES BY THE_____ AND SIPPED ON
                              NOUN   ADJECTIVE   NOUN

_____ _____. SUDDENLY, A LOUD_____ ECHOED THROUGH THE_____, MAKING EVERYONE_____
ADJECTIVE NOUN   NOUN   NOUN   VERB

IN THEIR SEATS.

ONE OF THE FRIENDS,_____, DECIDED TO_____ THE NOISE AND BRAVELY VENTURED INTO THE_____ THEY
                    NAME   VERB   NOUN

DISCOVERED A HIDDEN_____ COVERED IN_____ _____. _____ CAUTIOUSLY APPROACHED THE_____
                    NOUN   ADJECTIVE NOUN   NAME   NOUN

AND FOUND A_____ _____ SITTING ON AN OLD_____.
           ADJECTIVE NOUN   NOUN

AS_____ REACHED FOR THE_____, IT SUDDENLY_____ TO LIFE, ITS_____ GLOWING WITH AN EERIE
  NAME   NOUN   VERB   NOUN

_____ LIGHT. IT BEGAN TO_____ A_____ THAT TOLD A_____ TALE OF A_____ _____ THAT
ADJECTIVE   VERB   NOUN   ADJECTIVE   ADJECTIVE NOUN

_____ IN THE_____ _____. THE FRIENDS WERE_____ AND_____ AS THE_____
VERB   ADJECTIVE NOUN   ADJECTIVE   ADJECTIVE   NOUN

CONTINUED.

DETERMINED TO UNCOVER THE_____ _____, THE FRIENDS EMBARKED ON A_____ ADVENTURE THROUGH THE
                       ADJECTIVE NOUN   ADJECTIVE

_____. ALONG THE WAY, THEY ENCOUNTERED_____ _____ _____ AND EVEN A_____ THAT SEEMED TO
NOUN   NUMBER ADJECTIVE NOUN   NOUN

_____ WITH_____ _____. AT THE HEART OF THE_____, THEY FOUND A_____ _____ THAT
VERB   ADJECTIVE NOUN   NOUN   ADJECTIVE NOUN

_____ WITH_____ _____. IT WAS THE KEY TO BREAKING THE_____ _____ AND_____ THE
VERB   ADJECTIVE NOUN   ADJECTIVE NOUN   VERB

_____ _____ TO REST ONCE AND FOR ALL. WITH GREAT_____, THEY_____ THE_____, AND THE
ADJECTIVE NOUN   NOUN   VERB   NOUN

_____ _____ AWAY, LEAVING THE_____ IN PEACE. THE FRIENDS RETURNED TO THE_____ AND CELEBRATED
NOUN   VERB   NOUN   NOUN

THEIR_____ VICTORY WITH_____ _____ AND_____.
     ADJECTIVE   ADJECTIVE NOUN   NOUN

AS THE_____ SUBSIDED, THEY KNEW THAT THIS WOULD BE A_____ HALLOWEEN THEY WOULD NEVER FORGET, FULL OF
       NOUN   ADJECTIVE

_____ _____ AND_____ _____.
ADJECTIVE NOUN   ADJECTIVE NOUN

HANGMAN

WORD: _____

A B C D E F G H I J K L M N
O P Q R S T U V W X Y Z

WORD: _____

A B C D E F G H I J K L M N
O P Q R S T U V W X Y Z

WORD: _____

A B C D E F G H I J K L M N
O P Q R S T U V W X Y Z

WORD: _____

A B C D E F G H I J K L M N
O P Q R S T U V W X Y Z

WORD: _____

A B C D E F G H I J K L M N
O P Q R S T U V W X Y Z

RIP

WORD: _____

A B C D E F G H I J K L M N
O P Q R S T U V W X Y Z

BONE CHILLING MAZE
3

START

FINISH

WORD SEARCH 3

HALLOWEEN

```
Y M X R E E M U V G H C T I W
E X T W T Q K N C G R U N X V
D X H K A L O D R E Z R O E Q
P N M S E R O D E O E H R O H
O C P I N E E P M T O E D Y Z
L K B Q T U Y B N C N X L T L
J H O A G E I A O I I U U H X
G Z Y Z G E L S T T K P A G A
H Y Y X V O T W E J C P C H E
T E D E K U F Y L M V O M Z R
K Q N C M J V K E F A A C U I
I T A E R T R O K C I R T E P
E J C X R Y Y O S B M E L J M
S M Y W P N Y P V V B Y W L A
Y W J O D B T S O H G P G Y V
```

CANDY	HAUNTED	SPOOKY
CAULDRON	JACK-O'-LANTERN	TRICK-OR-TREAT
COSTUME	OCTOBER	VAMPIRE
CREEPY	PUMPKIN	WITCH
GHOST	SKELETON	ZOMBIE

WOULD YOU RATHER...

HAVE TO WEAR A SPOOKY GHOST COSTUME EVERY DAY FOR A MONTH
LEADING UP TO HALLOWEEN

OR

ONLY EAT CANDY CORN FOR A WEEK STRAIGHT

• •

GO TO SCHOOL ON HALLOWEEN DRESSED AS A MUMMY WITH TOILET PAPER
UNRAVELING ALL DAY

OR

WEAR A COSTUME THAT MAKES YOU LOOK LIKE A GIANT CANDY BAR AND BE
CHASED BY KIDS

• •

HAVE TO COMMUNICATE ONLY IN SPOOKY GHOST SOUNDS

OR

TALK LIKE A PIRATE FOR THE ENTIRE HALLOWEEN SEASON

• •

HAVE A PUMPKIN PIE-SCENTED PERFUME

OR

A COSTUME THAT MAKES YOU LOOK LIKE A HUMAN-SIZED CANDY BAR

PUMPKIN CARVING

CREATE YOUR OWN JACK-O'-LANTERN

HANGMAN

WORD: _____

ABCDEFGHIJKLMN
OPQRSTUVWXYZ

WORD: _____

ABCDEFGHIJKLMN
OPQRSTUVWXYZ

WORD: _____

ABCDEFGHIJKLMN
OPQRSTUVWXYZ

WORD: _____

ABCDEFGHIJKLMN
OPQRSTUVWXYZ

WORD: _____

ABCDEFGHIJKLMN
OPQRSTUVWXYZ

WORD: _____

ABCDEFGHIJKLMN
OPQRSTUVWXYZ

RIP

MYSTIC M.A.S.H.

MANSION-APARTMENT- SHACK-HOUSE

MONSTER SPOUSE
1. _____
2. _____
3. _____
4. _____
5. _____

HAUNTED HOUSE LOCATION
1. _____
2. _____
3. _____
4. _____
5. _____

SPOOKY TRANSPORTATION
1. _____
2. _____
3. _____
4. _____
5. _____

CREEPY CRAWLY PET
1. _____
2. _____
3. _____
4. _____
5. _____

NUMBER OF KIDS
1. _____
2. _____
3. _____
4. _____
5. _____

FUTURE MORBID JOB
1. _____
2. _____
3. _____
4. _____
5. _____

SPIRAL CIRCLE

YOUR MAGIC NUMBER

WICKED WORDPLAY

ON A CREEPY HALLOWEEN NIGHT, _____ FRIENDS GATHERED FOR A SPOOKY SLUMBER PARTY
                             NUMBER

AT A HAUNTED HOUSE. THEY WORE _____ AND WERE READY FOR A NIGHT OF EERIE FUN.
                              COSTUMES

AS THEY SETTLED IN, THEY HEARD STRANGE NOISES FROM THE ATTIC. THEY BRAVELY WENT UP AND

FOUND A _____ THAT OPENED TO A _____ WORLD WITH _____ . THEY
        NOUN   ADJECTIVE   PLURAL NOUN

ENCOUNTERED _____ WITCHES, _____ GHOSTS, AND A TALKING CAT.
            ADJECTIVE   ADJECTIVE

THEY SOLVED RIDDLES, PLAYED GAMES, AND EARNED _____ TREATS. WHEN THEY RETURNED,
                                              ADJECTIVE

ONLY _____ MINUTES HAD PASSED, BUT THEY HAD _____ TALES TO SHARE.
     NUMBER   ADJECTIVE

BACK AT THE SLUMBER PARTY, THEY PLAYED _____ GAMES, SNACKED ON _____ , AND
                                       ADJECTIVE   PLURAL NOUN

STAYED UP ALL NIGHT, CREATING _____ MEMORIES.
                              ADJECTIVE

IT WAS A HALLOWEEN NIGHT THEY'D NEVER FORGET, FILLED WITH _____ ADVENTURES AND
                                                          ADJECTIVE

_____ .
NOUN

WORD SEARCH 4

WITCHES

```
H P A M W G G U T P M Z J
U O K I P O F R W W Y N V
T A C K C A L B Y L V C J
N C I U O R P L Q H O B K
A S T V S O U G E N G V Y
H H S B T P B X J P B R W
C Z M I F W O U E E S A K
N M O T F A R C H C T I W
E N O W G E L M U D R L J
V Y R E C R O S W S A I F
O R B P Q X P E S F W M T
C D P O J S G J V U B A N
Q B H R Z F U U Y G S F L
```

BLACK CAT	ENCHANT	SORCERY
BOOK	FAMILIAR	SPELL
BROOMSTICK	HEX	WART
CONJURE	HOCUS-POCUS	WICCA
COVEN	POTION	WITCHCRAFT

CATEGORIES GAME

LETTER	MONSTER	COSTUME	SCENERY	MOVIE	CANDY	SCORE

NUMBER OF ROUNDS

TOTAL SCORE

HANGMAN

WORD: _____

A B C D E F G H I J K L M N
O P Q R S T U V W X Y Z

WORD: _____

A B C D E F G H I J K L M N
O P Q R S T U V W X Y Z

WORD: _____

A B C D E F G H I J K L M N
O P Q R S T U V W X Y Z

WORD: _____

A B C D E F G H I J K L M N
O P Q R S T U V W X Y Z

WORD: _____

A B C D E F G H I J K L M N
O P Q R S T U V W X Y Z

WORD: _____

A B C D E F G H I J K L M N
O P Q R S T U V W X Y Z

RIP

WOULD YOU RATHER....

HAVE A BROOMSTICK THAT FLIES ONLY TWO FEET OFF THE GROUND

OR

A MAGIC CAULDRON THAT ONLY BREWS PEANUT BUTTER AND JELLY SANDWICHES

. . . .

HAVE YOUR CANDY STASH REPLACED WITH VEGETABLES

OR

HAVE YOUR PUMPKIN CARVING TURN INTO A GIANT PUMPKIN PIE

. . . .

ATTEND A COSTUME PARTY WITH A STRICT "NO COSTUMES" RULE

OR

GO TRICK-OR-TREATING IN A NEIGHBORHOOD WHERE EVERYONE GIVES OUT BROCCOLI INSTEAD OF CANDY

. . . .

HAVE A PET BLACK CAT THAT BRINGS YOU GOOD LUCK ON HALLOWEEN BUT BAD LUCK THE REST OF THE YEAR

OR

A PET GHOST THAT'S INVISIBLE BUT LOVES TO PLAY PRANKS

MYSTIC M.A.S.H.

MANSION-APARTMENT- SHACK-HOUSE

MONSTER SPOUSE

1. _____
2. _____
3. _____
4. _____
5. _____

HAUNTED HOUSE LOCATION

1. _____
2. _____
3. _____
4. _____
5. _____

SPOOKY TRANSPORTATION

1. _____
2. _____
3. _____
4. _____
5. _____

CREEPY CRAWLY PET

1. _____
2. _____
3. _____
4. _____
5. _____

NUMBER OF KIDS

1. _____
2. _____
3. _____
4. _____
5. _____

FUTURE MORBID JOB

1. _____
2. _____
3. _____
4. _____
5. _____

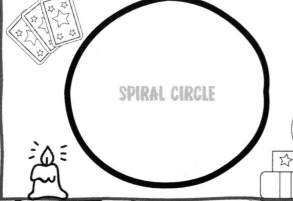

SPIRAL CIRCLE

YOUR MAGIC NUMBER

PUMPKIN CARVING

CREATE YOUR OWN JACK-O'-LANTERN

WORD SEARCH 5

VAMPIRE

W	R	Z	M	Y	S	E	D	T	D	N	R	I
C	G	H	Y	T	G	L	A	N	R	E	T	E
L	I	O	H	I	K	K	V	V	K	K	S	I
N	L	A	P	L	D	S	C	C	B	A	R	F
I	Q	Y	L	A	A	M	U	H	E	T	I	B
Q	O	E	F	T	E	S	T	D	Z	S	H	T
I	Q	R	Y	R	D	I	A	H	I	U	T	C
L	J	U	J	O	N	R	R	S	G	N	A	F
L	E	A	O	M	U	I	E	T	Q	I	B	Z
G	D	L	O	M	Q	P	F	T	B	I	N	A
L	B	I	V	I	R	M	S	F	N	Q	X	D
I	H	Q	M	H	Q	A	O	O	O	U	D	G
M	R	S	K	Y	E	V	N	U	K	C	H	N

BAT	ETERNAL	NOSFERATU
BITE	FANGS	STAKE
BLOODSUCKER	HUNTER	THIRST
COFFIN	IMMORTALITY	UNDEAD
DUSK	NIGHT	VAMPIRISM

MEDIUM

Top-left puzzle

7	2		4			5		
3	1	4	2		9			
	8			7		2	4	3
5	9	2	6			7	3	1
	3	1	5		7		6	
6		8	3		1	4	5	
	6	7			3	8		4
		3		7	2	5	9	
1	5		8	6			2	

Top-right puzzle

4			1	7	2			
8	9			4	2			5
	1		9		5	6		
6			4	2			5	
9	5		6	1			4	2
		4				3	1	9
	4	8		9	6		3	1
5	7			3		4	6	8
	3		5	4	8	7	2	

Bottom-left puzzle

6		2		4	7			3
3	5			7	2	4		
	4	7	2	3	1	8	6	
	7			5	6			1
	2	3	8	1	6	9		4
	6			4		5		
8				9				2
		4	1		2			6
2	1		3		8	4		7

Bottom-right puzzle

7	8		2	3			5	4
		4			5	1	7	
2	1			7	9		6	3
3	9		8		6			7
		2	9		7		8	6
8	6			4				9
4			7	9	8			
1	5	9	3				2	8
6	7		1			2	4	9

WOULD YOU RATHER...

SPEND HALLOWEEN NIGHT EXPLORING A HAUNTED HOUSE WITH YOUR FRIENDS

OR

GO ON A SPOOKY GRAVEYARD TOUR WITH A PROFESSIONAL GHOST HUNTER

• •

ATTEND A COSTUME PARTY DRESSED AS YOUR FAVORITE FICTIONAL VILLAIN

OR

SPEND HALLOWEEN NIGHT WATCHING HORROR MOVIES ALONE IN A DARK, CREEPY FOREST CABIN

• •

HAVE THE POWER TO COMMUNICATE WITH GHOSTS AND HAVE A CONVERSATION WITH A FAMOUS HISTORICAL FIGURE WHO'S PASSED AWAY ON HALLOWEEN,

OR

BE THE STAR OF A POPULAR HALLOWEEN-THEMED REALITY TV SHOW FOR A YEAR

• •

HAVE THE ABILITY TO INSTANTLY CREATE ANY HALLOWEEN COSTUME YOU CAN IMAGINE, NO MATTER HOW COMPLEX,

OR

BE ABLE TO VISIT ANY HAUNTED LOCATION IN THE WORLD FOR A NIGHT BUT NOT BE ABLE TO TELL ANYONE ABOUT YOUR EXPERIENCE

MYSTIC M.A.S.H.

MANSION-APARTMENT- SHACK-HOUSE

MONSTER SPOUSE

1. _____
2. _____
3. _____
4. _____
5. _____

HAUNTED HOUSE LOCATION

1. _____
2. _____
3. _____
4. _____
5. _____

SPOOKY TRANSPORTATION

1. _____
2. _____
3. _____
4. _____
5. _____

CREEPY CRAWLY PET

1. _____
2. _____
3. _____
4. _____
5. _____

NUMBER OF KIDS

1. _____
2. _____
3. _____
4. _____
5. _____

FUTURE MORBID JOB

1. _____
2. _____
3. _____
4. _____
5. _____

SPIRAL CIRCLE

YOUR MAGIC NUMBER

WORD SEARCH 6

FAMILY MOVIE NIGHT

```
B P Y Q S U C O P S U C O H
E E D I R B E S P R O C P T
E E I N E E W N E K N A R F
T I X F T G R E M L I N S Y
L E X X S E H C T I W E H T
E R X Y N A M R O N A R A P
J E S U O H R E T S N O M D
U P B J M S V F V C Y M X E
I S S R E T S U B T S O H G
C A O H L S C O O B Y D O O
E C M K T G N S N B N G F Z
H A U N T E D M A N S I O N
O G Y L I M A F S M A D D A
T E N I L A R O C V X P G V
```

ADDAMS FAMILY	FRANKENWEENIE	LITTLE MONSTERS
BEETLEJUICE	GHOSTBUSTERS	MONSTER HOUSE
CASPER	GREMLINS	PARANORMAN
CORALINE	HAUNTED MANSION	SCOOBY DOO
CORPSE BRIDE	HOCUS POCUS	THE WITCHES

CATEGORIES GAME

LETTER	MONSTER	COSTUME	SCENERY	MOVIE	CANDY	SCORE

NUMBER OF ROUNDS

TOTAL SCORE

CARVE THE PUMPKIN MAZE 4

START

FINISH

WORD SEARCH 7
WEREWOLF

```
I W A T A S E U D B L K J N
V Q G E U M M L W T A C O I
G D U M X T A F S R L I S T
S Y U M N X I U G D T N U H
Z X Y P O R H T N A C Y L A
U N E M M O M C M I Z Q R L
B A Q D S J D R E V L I S Q
D F N K C O O E A T K W Y Y
L M Z J J F D G S A I C O Z
S G N E S F J N S R L B A H
D A M N L M H U E A U V T P
I L A R E F U H W V G C C C
Y R E T F I H S E P A H S M
T H G I L N O O M L L U F P
```

BITE	FUR	MOONLIGHT
CLAWS	HOWLING	PACK
CURSED	HUNGER	SHAPE-SHIFTER
FERAL	HUNT	SILVER
FULL MOON	LYCANTHROPY	TRANSFORMATION

WICKED WORDPLAY

ONCE UPON A _____ FALL SEASON, A GROUP OF_____ DARING TEENS EMBARKED ON A CAMPING TRIP DEEP WITHIN THE
                    ADJECTIVE   NUMBER

_____ WOODS. WITH THEIR_____ BACKPACKS AND A_____ OF MARSHMALLOWS, THEY WERE READY FOR A
ADJECTIVE   ADJECTIVE   NOUN

THRILLING ADVENTURE.

AS THEY SET UP CAMP BY THE_____ LAKE, THEY NOTICED THE TREES CASTING_____ SHADOWS IN THE_____
                         ADJECTIVE   ADJECTIVE   ADJECTIVE

MOONLIGHT. THE WIND WHISPERED THROUGH THE_____ , AND AN EERIE_____ FOG ROLLED IN.
                                         NOUN   ADJECTIVE

AROUND THE _____ , THEY GATHERED TO TELL_____ GHOST STORIES THAT MADE THEIR_____ HAIR STAND ON
           NOUN   ADJECTIVE   NOUN

END. SUDDENLY, THEY HEARD A_____ NOISE IN THE_____ BUSHES NEARBY.
                           ADJECTIVE   NOUN

WITH _____ IN HAND, THEY VENTURED INTO THE_____ DARKNESS. THEIR FLASHLIGHT REVEALED_____ EYES
     NOUN   ADJECTIVE   ADJECTIVE

GLEAMING FROM THE_____ , BUT IT TURNED OUT TO BE A _____ FOX SCAVENGING FOR FOOD.
                 NOUN   ADJECTIVE

RELIEVED, THEY RETURNED TO THEIR CAMPFIRE, ROASTING MARSHMALLOWS AND SAVORING THE_____ TASTE OF VICTORY
                                                                                ADJECTIVE

OVER THE_____ UNKNOWN.
        ADJECTIVE

AS THEY SETTLED INTO THEIR SLEEPING BAGS, THE_____ BREEZE CARRIED THE DISTANT HOWLS OF_____ WOLVES. THE
                                             NOUN   ADJECTIVE

TEENS DRIFTED OFF TO SLEEP, EMBRACING THE EERIE CHARM OF THEIR FALL CAMPING ADVENTURE.

IT WAS A NIGHT THEY'D_____ AND CHERISH, FILLED WITH _____ THRILLS AND THE MAGIC OF THE FALL SEASON..
                     VERB   NOUN

HARD

Puzzle 1 (top-left):

1		7				6		
		4	7	9			3	
	5	3	1		4	9		7
	1	8	4		3			
			6	8		3		
	3	9	7	5				8
	7	2			6		1	
	8		3		5	4	7	6
	4		9			8		

Puzzle 2 (top-right):

		8		2		3		
	9	2		3				7
1		3			9		2	
9	5	3			2			
		4	3			8	5	2
2	8	6				7	4	
	6	9		7	3		8	
	7					8	2	6
	2					4		3

  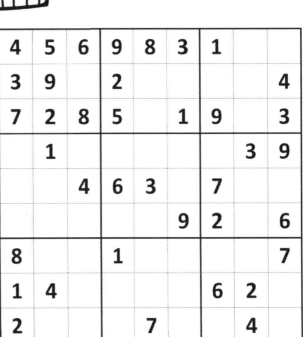

Puzzle 3 (bottom-left):

	6	8		2		9	1	4
4					6			
5		9				3	6	
9		7						6
		4	2	7		5	3	8
8	3	2	6	4	5			
		4				7	8	
2				9		4	5	
7			8	5				1

Puzzle 4 (bottom-right):

4	5	6	9	8	3	1		
3	9			2				4
7	2	8	5			1	9	3
	1						3	9
		4	6	3		7		
				9	2			6
8			1					7
1	4					6	2	
2			7					4

MYSTIC M.A.S.H.

MANSION-APARTMENT- SHACK-HOUSE

MONSTER SPOUSE

1. _____
2. _____
3. _____
4. _____
5. _____

HAUNTED HOUSE LOCATION

1. _____
2. _____
3. _____
4. _____
5. _____

SPOOKY TRANSPORTATION

1. _____
2. _____
3. _____
4. _____
5. _____

CREEPY CRAWLY PET

1. _____
2. _____
3. _____
4. _____
5. _____

NUMBER OF KIDS

1. _____
2. _____
3. _____
4. _____
5. _____

FUTURE MORBID JOB

1. _____
2. _____
3. _____
4. _____
5. _____

SPIRAL CIRCLE

YOUR MAGIC NUMBER

WORD SEARCH 8

GHOST

```
N P A R A N O R M A L Y T
M O T N A H P C L L L R S
T X I S T T V L Y D A E P
N K R T S I Y U L N R T O
N W I V I A B R S K U C O
I V P G E R O P H A T E K
M I S F G W A A D Y A P Y
X E C M R R U P L N N S F
P T D E E N T D P N R Z V
V I H N T I U B I A E R D
I T T I L C R L G C P H E
O T N K O N E E S N U G C
Z G D O P T U R E U S I M
```

APPARITION	PHANTOM	SUPERNATURAL
EERIE	POLTERGEIST	TRANSPARENT
HAUNTING	SPECTER	UNCANNY
OTHERWORLDLY	SPIRIT	UNSEEN
PARANORMAL	SPOOKY	WRAITH

HANGMAN

WORD: _____

ABCDEFGHIJKLMN
OPQRSTUVWXYZ

WORD: _____

ABCDEFGHIJKLMN
OPQRSTUVWXYZ

WORD: _____

ABCDEFGHIJKLMN
OPQRSTUVWXYZ

WORD: _____

ABCDEFGHIJKLMN
OPQRSTUVWXYZ

WORD: _____

ABCDEFGHIJKLMN
OPQRSTUVWXYZ

RIP

WORD: _____

ABCDEFGHIJKLMN
OPQRSTUVWXYZ

CATEGORIES GAME

LETTER	MONSTER	COSTUME	SCENERY	MOVIE	CANDY	SCORE

NUMBER OF ROUNDS

TOTAL SCORE

MYSTIC M.A.S.H.

MANSION-APARTMENT- SHACK-HOUSE

MONSTER SPOUSE
1. _____
2. _____
3. _____
4. _____
5. _____

HAUNTED HOUSE LOCATION
1. _____
2. _____
3. _____
4. _____
5. _____

SPOOKY TRANSPORTATION
1. _____
2. _____
3. _____
4. _____
5. _____

CREEPY CRAWLY PET
1. _____
2. _____
3. _____
4. _____
5. _____

NUMBER OF KIDS
1. _____
2. _____
3. _____
4. _____
5. _____

FUTURE MORBID JOB
1. _____
2. _____
3. _____
4. _____
5. _____

SPIRAL CIRCLE

YOUR MAGIC NUMBER

SOLUTIONS

EASY SOLUTIONS

Grid 1

9	8	6	1	7	5	3	4	2
4	3	7	9	6	2	5	8	1
1	5	2	4	8	3	7	6	9
6	4	8	3	5	1	2	9	7
2	9	3	6	4	7	1	5	8
5	7	1	8	2	9	4	3	6
7	1	9	5	3	6	8	2	4
3	6	4	2	1	8	9	7	5
8	2	5	7	9	4	6	1	3

Grid 2

8	2	9	3	5	7	6	1	4
7	3	5	1	4	6	2	8	9
1	6	4	2	9	8	5	7	3
4	5	3	8	1	9	7	2	6
2	1	8	7	6	4	3	9	5
9	7	6	5	2	3	1	4	8
6	9	2	4	7	5	8	3	1
3	4	7	6	8	1	9	5	2
5	8	1	9	3	2	4	6	7

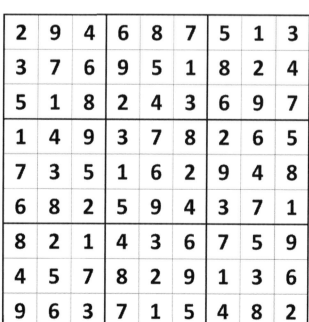

Grid 3

9	8	1	2	4	3	7	5	6
6	7	4	5	9	8	2	3	1
3	2	5	6	7	1	8	9	4
2	4	7	8	6	5	3	1	9
5	9	6	1	3	7	4	2	8
8	1	3	4	2	9	6	7	5
1	6	2	3	5	4	9	8	7
7	3	8	9	1	6	5	4	2
4	5	9	7	8	2	1	6	3

Grid 4

2	9	4	6	8	7	5	1	3
3	7	6	9	5	1	8	2	4
5	1	8	2	4	3	6	9	7
1	4	9	3	7	8	2	6	5
7	3	5	1	6	2	9	4	8
6	8	2	5	9	4	3	7	1
8	2	1	4	3	6	7	5	9
4	5	7	8	2	9	1	3	6
9	6	3	7	1	5	4	8	2

MEDIUM SOLUTIONS

Grid 1

7	2	6	4	3	5	1	8	9
3	1	4	2	8	9	6	7	5
9	8	5	7	1	6	2	4	3
5	9	2	6	4	8	7	3	1
4	3	1	5	2	7	9	6	8
6	7	8	3	9	1	4	5	2
2	6	7	9	5	3	8	1	4
8	4	3	1	7	2	5	9	6
1	5	9	8	6	4	3	2	7

Grid 2

4	6	5	1	7	2	9	8	3
8	9	7	3	6	4	2	1	5
3	1	2	9	8	5	6	7	4
6	8	1	4	2	9	3	5	7
9	5	3	6	1	7	8	4	2
7	2	4	8	5	3	1	9	6
2	4	8	7	9	6	5	3	1
5	7	9	2	3	1	4	6	8
1	3	6	5	4	8	7	2	9

Grid 3

6	8	2	5	9	4	7	1	3
3	5	1	6	8	7	2	4	9
9	4	7	2	3	1	8	6	5
4	7	8	9	2	5	6	3	1
5	2	3	8	1	6	9	7	4
1	6	9	7	4	3	5	2	8
8	3	6	4	7	9	1	5	2
7	9	4	1	5	2	3	8	6
2	1	5	3	6	8	4	9	7

Grid 4

7	8	6	2	3	1	9	5	4
9	4	3	6	8	5	1	7	2
2	1	5	4	7	9	8	6	3
3	9	1	8	2	6	5	4	7
5	2	4	9	1	7	3	8	6
8	6	7	5	4	3	2	9	1
4	3	2	7	9	8	6	1	5
1	5	9	3	6	4	7	2	8
6	7	8	1	5	2	4	3	9

1	9	7	2	3	8	6	4	5
2	6	4	5	7	9	8	3	1
8	5	3	1	6	4	9	2	7
6	1	8	4	9	3	7	5	2
7	2	5	6	8	1	3	9	4
4	3	9	7	5	2	1	6	8
3	7	2	8	4	6	5	1	9
9	8	1	3	2	5	4	7	6
5	4	6	9	1	7	2	8	3

4	7	8	6	2	5	3	9	1
6	9	2	8	3	1	5	4	7
1	3	5	7	4	9	6	2	8
9	5	3	4	8	2	7	1	6
7	1	4	3	9	6	8	5	2
2	8	6	1	5	7	4	3	9
5	6	9	2	7	3	1	8	4
3	4	7	9	1	8	2	6	5
8	2	1	5	6	4	9	7	3

3	6	8	5	2	7	9	1	4
4	7	1	9	3	6	8	2	5
5	2	9	1	8	4	3	6	7
9	5	7	3	1	8	2	4	6
6	1	4	2	7	9	5	3	8
8	3	2	6	4	5	1	7	9
1	9	5	4	6	3	7	8	2
2	8	6	7	9	1	4	5	3
7	4	3	8	5	2	6	9	1

4	5	6	9	8	3	1	7	2
3	9	1	2	6	7	8	5	4
7	2	8	5	4	1	9	6	3
6	1	2	7	5	8	4	3	9
9	8	4	6	3	2	7	1	5
5	7	3	4	1	9	2	8	6
8	6	5	1	2	4	3	9	7
1	4	7	3	9	5	6	2	8
2	3	9	8	7	6	5	4	1

MAZE SOLUTIONS

1

2

3

4

WORD SEARCH SOLUTIONS

1

S	T	C	Z	E	G	D	U	R	G	E	H	T	E
U	T	U	W	Q	L	X	J	M	H	C	W	U	Q
H	E	G	O	E	M	Q	N	T	Z	A	U	O	N
M	Y	N	S	L	O	I	A	N	G	L	U	S	L
U	A	I	R	L	Q	E	M	A	H	P	J	T	N
Q	L	R	E	E	R	S	Y	N	T	T	V	H	H
R	P	U	H	B	E	N	D	G	V	E	F	G	F
L	E	J	T	A	T	E	N	I	R	I	I	I	N
B	M	N	O	N	A	S	A	L	G	U	W	L	Q
O	O	O	E	N	W	H	C	A	C	Q	V	Q	T
D	C	C	H	A	K	T	Y	M	O	M	Q	L	M
Z	L	V	T	U	R	X	T	H	E	R	I	N	G
P	A	Z	G	X	A	I	M	F	R	E	A	K	Y
X	W	R	L	U	D	S	U	P	M	A	R	K	I

2

S	U	N	T	W	J	M	W	X	Y	N	L	A	P
P	U	D	L	C	L	M	O	T	N	A	H	P	O
O	T	P	C	K	A	B	E	I	R	E	E	P	S
O	G	P	X	K	M	T	L	U	Y	Y	E	A	S
K	W	S	B	I	R	M	T	S	O	H	G	R	E
Y	O	T	G	D	O	A	A	A	A	I	O	I	S
G	O	I	D	E	N	O	D	N	A	B	A	T	S
U	N	R	B	R	A	H	Y	S	H	R	U	I	I
T	S	I	E	G	R	E	T	L	O	P	M	O	O
F	V	P	K	W	A	K	E	X	D	A	L	N	N
K	U	S	N	A	P	H	A	U	N	T	I	N	G
S	U	O	I	R	E	T	S	Y	M	R	B	W	E
I	P	F	Z	S	O	R	B	C	N	R	V	W	C
U	S	R	H	K	K	W	C	I	N	O	M	E	D

3

Y	M	X	R	E	E	M	U	V	G	H	C	T	I	W
E	X	T	W	T	Q	K	N	C	G	R	U	N	X	V
D	X	H	K	A	L	O	D	R	E	Z	R	O	E	Q
P	N	M	S	E	R	O	D	E	O	E	H	R	O	H
O	C	P	I	N	E	E	P	M	T	O	E	D	Y	Z
L	K	B	Q	T	U	Y	B	N	C	N	X	L	T	L
J	H	O	A	G	E	I	A	O	I	I	U	U	H	X
G	Z	Y	Z	G	E	L	S	T	T	K	P	A	G	A
H	Y	Y	X	V	O	T	W	E	J	C	P	C	H	E
T	E	D	E	K	U	F	Y	L	M	V	O	M	Z	R
K	Q	N	C	M	J	V	K	E	F	A	A	C	U	I
I	T	A	E	R	T	R	O	K	C	I	R	T	E	P
E	J	C	X	R	Y	Y	O	S	B	M	E	L	J	M
S	M	Y	W	P	N	Y	P	V	V	B	Y	W	L	A
Y	W	J	O	D	B	T	S	O	H	G	P	G	Y	V

4

H	P	A	M	W	G	G	U	T	P	M	Z	J
U	O	K	I	P	O	F	R	W	W	Y	N	V
T	A	C	K	C	A	L	B	Y	L	V	C	J
N	C	I	U	O	R	P	L	Q	H	O	B	K
A	S	T	V	S	O	U	G	E	N	G	V	Y
H	H	S	B	T	P	B	X	J	P	B	R	W
C	Z	M	I	F	W	O	U	E	E	S	A	K
N	M	O	T	F	A	R	C	H	C	T	I	W
E	N	O	W	G	E	L	M	U	D	R	L	J
V	Y	R	E	C	R	O	S	W	S	A	I	F
O	R	B	P	Q	X	P	E	S	F	W	M	T
C	D	P	O	J	S	G	J	V	U	B	A	N
Q	B	H	R	Z	F	U	U	Y	G	S	F	L

5

W	R	Z	M	Y	S	E	D	T	D	N	R	I
C	G	H	Y	T	G	L	A	N	R	E	T	E
L	I	O	H	I	K	K	V	Y	K	K	S	I
N	L	A	P	L	D	S	C	C	B	A	R	F
I	Q	Y	L	A	A	M	U	H	E	T	I	B
Q	O	E	F	T	E	S	T	D	Z	S	H	T
I	Q	R	Y	R	D	I	A	H	I	U	T	C
L	J	U	J	O	N	R	R	S	G	N	A	F
L	E	A	O	M	U	I	E	T	Q	I	B	Z
G	D	L	O	M	Q	P	F	T	B	I	N	A
L	B	I	V	I	R	M	S	F	N	Q	X	D
I	H	Q	M	H	Q	A	O	O	O	U	D	G
M	R	S	K	Y	E	V	N	U	K	C	H	N

6

B	P	Y	Q	S	U	C	O	P	S	U	C	O	H
E	E	D	I	R	B	E	S	P	R	O	C	P	T
E	E	I	N	E	E	W	N	E	K	N	A	R	F
T	I	X	F	T	G	R	E	M	L	I	N	S	Y
L	E	X	X	S	E	H	C	T	I	W	E	H	T
E	R	X	Y	N	A	M	R	O	N	A	R	A	P
J	E	S	U	O	H	R	E	T	S	N	O	M	D
U	P	B	J	M	S	V	F	V	C	Y	M	X	E
I	S	S	R	E	T	S	U	B	T	S	O	H	G
C	A	O	H	L	S	C	O	O	B	Y	D	O	O
E	C	M	K	T	G	N	S	N	B	N	G	F	Z
H	A	U	N	T	E	D	M	A	N	S	I	O	N
O	G	Y	L	I	M	A	F	S	M	A	D	D	A
T	E	N	I	L	A	R	O	C	V	X	P	G	V

7

I	W	A	T	A	S	E	U	D	B	L	K	J	N
V	Q	G	E	U	M	M	L	W	T	A	C	O	I
G	D	U	M	X	T	A	F	S	R	L	I	S	T
S	Y	M	N	X	I	U	G	O	D	T	N	U	H
Z	X	Y	P	O	R	H	T	N	A	C	Y	L	A
U	N	E	M	M	O	M	C	M	I	Z	Q	R	L
B	A	Q	D	S	J	D	R	E	V	L	I	S	Q
D	F	N	K	C	O	O	E	A	T	K	W	Y	Y
L	M	Z	J	J	F	D	G	S	A	I	C	O	Z
S	G	N	E	S	F	J	N	S	R	L	B	A	H
D	A	M	N	L	M	H	U	E	A	U	V	T	P
I	L	A	R	E	F	U	H	W	V	G	C	C	C
Y	R	E	T	F	I	H	S	E	P	A	H	S	M
T	H	G	I	L	N	O	O	M	L	L	U	F	P

8

N	P	A	R	A	N	O	R	M	A	L	Y	T
M	O	T	N	A	H	P	C	L	L	L	R	S
T	X	I	S	T	T	V	L	Y	D	A	E	P
N	K	R	T	S	I	Y	U	L	N	R	T	O
N	W	I	V	I	A	B	R	S	K	U	C	O
I	V	P	G	E	R	O	P	H	A	T	E	K
M	I	S	F	G	W	A	A	D	Y	A	P	Y
X	E	C	M	R	R	U	P	L	N	N	S	F
P	T	D	E	E	N	T	D	P	N	R	Z	V
V	I	H	N	T	I	U	B	I	A	E	R	D
I	T	T	I	L	C	R	L	G	C	P	H	E
O	T	N	K	O	N	E	E	S	N	U	G	C
Z	G	D	O	P	T	U	R	E	U	S	I	M

Made in the USA
Las Vegas, NV
28 October 2024